KU-475-476

Mighty Machines

DIGGERS

Amanda Askew

QED Publishing

Words in **bold** can be found
in the Glossary on page 23.

Copyright © QED Publishing 2010

First published in the UK in 2010 by
QED Publishing
A Quarto Group company
226 City Road
London EC1V 2TT

www.qed-publishing.co.uk

All rights reserved. No part of this publication may be reproduced,
stored in a retrieval system, or transmitted in any form or by any
means, electronic, mechanical, photocopying, recording, or otherwise,
without the permission of the publisher, nor be otherwise circulated
in any form of binding or cover other than that in which it is published
and without a similar condition being imposed on the subsequent purchaser.

A Catalogue record for this book is available from the British Library.

ISBN 978 1 84835 765 5

Written by Amanda Askew
Designed by Phil and Traci Morash (Fineline Studios)
Editor Angela Royston
Picture Researcher Maria Joannou

Printed in China

Picture credits
Key: t = top, b = bottom, c = centre, FC = front cover, BC = back cover

Alamy Images David Williams 17c, Mike Dobel 18–19, David R. Frazier Photolibrary Inc 21t;
Dreamstime Grazvydas 1, 6–7; **Getty Images** Liam Bailey 14b, 22br; **Istockphoto** Purdue9394 4–5,
Shaun Dodds 12, Sascha Rosenau Njaa 14–15, Shaun Dodds 22tr; **Photolibrary** Age Fotostock/Gary
Moon 9b, 22bl, Tips Italia/Bildagentur RM 10–11, Index Stock Imagery/Bill Keefrey 11t, Age Fotostock/
Javier Larrea 13, Imagebroker.net/Jochen Tack 20–21, Tips Italia/Bildagentur RM 22tl; **Shutterstock**
mg14008 FC, Sevda 4, Stanislav Komogorov 6, Jiri Slama 8–9, 22tc, GRAPIX BC; **U Mole** 16–17, 22bc
(Photos supplied by **U Mole**, a division of VP plc detailing MTS suction excavation equipment. For more
info visit www.umole.co.uk)

Contents

What is a digger?

A digger digs holes and trenches.
Diggers are also called excavators.
These machines are often used on **building sites**, with **loaders** and **bulldozers**.

A digger on wheels can go on the road
to get from one job to another.

Some diggers have big wheels. Other diggers run on tracks. Tracks stop the digger from sinking into the ground.

A digger with tracks is called a crawler. It can move over rough ground.

tracks

Parts of a **digger**

A digger has three main parts – a cab, an arm and an **attachment**. The attachment is usually a **bucket** with teeth. The bucket scoops up the soil and stones.

The driver sits in the cab and controls the digger.

tracks

arm

The arm of the digger joins the bucket or other attachment to the cab.

bucket attachment

driver's cab

Buckets

The bucket is at the end of the arm. Buckets are made of metal and come in many shapes and sizes. Each one does a different job.

The teeth on a bucket are large, but not sharp. They push through the ground, just like your teeth bite into food.

teeth

Some buckets are very wide. The driver uses a wide bucket to scrape up earth or stones.

A wide bucket collects lots of stones in each scoop.

Digging and moving

The digger is one of the most important machines on a building site. It digs up the ground and clears away any unwanted **rubble**.

grab

The grab clamps together to lift and hold the rubble.

A grab is like two buckets that bite together. A grab is used to lift and carry heavy objects, such as piles of rocks.

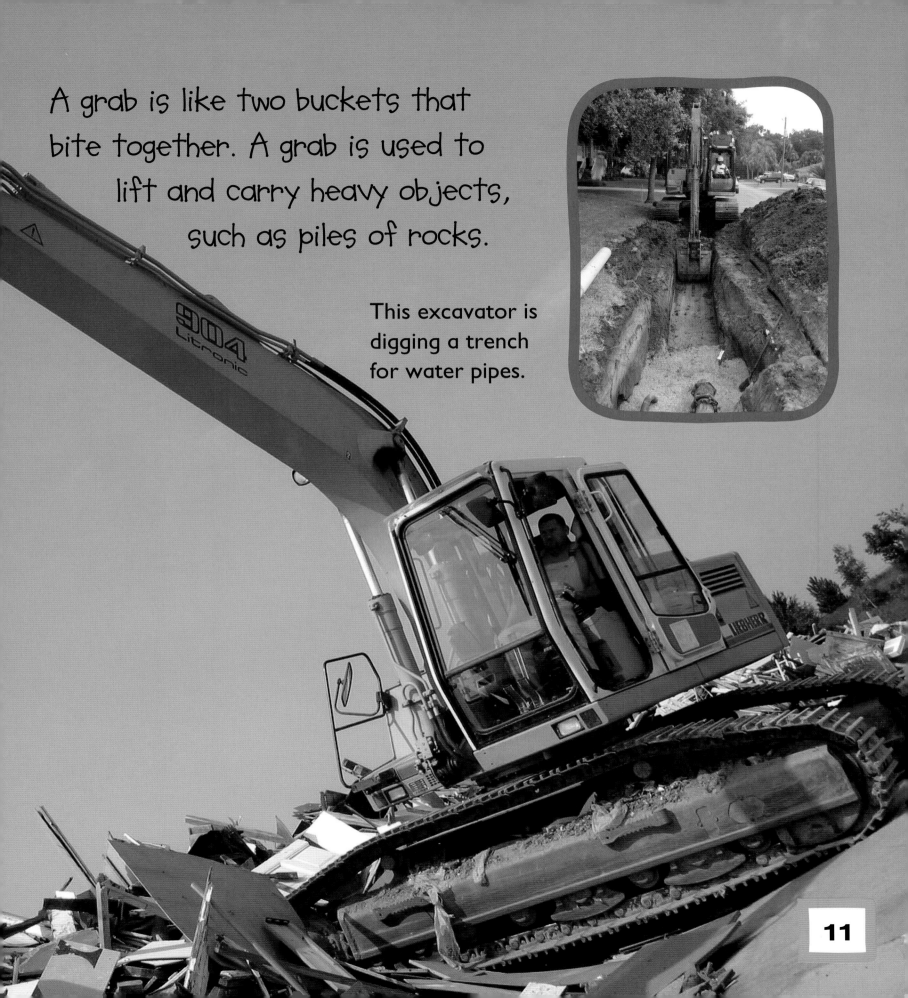

This excavator is digging a trench for water pipes.

Breaking up hard ground

Diggers can break through almost any ground, even frozen earth. This means that building work can carry on in almost any weather!

A ripper is used instead of a bucket. When the ripper crashes into the hard surface, it makes the ground crack.

The spike has to hit the ground over and over again to break up hard earth.

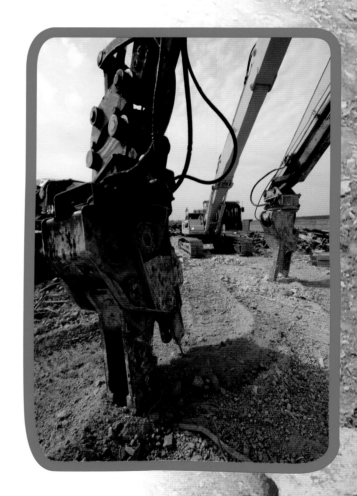

A ripper is a spike that is shaped like the letter V.

ripper

Demolition

Excavators can be used to knock down houses and small office blocks. This is called demolition. Excavators **demolish** a building safely, bit by bit.

Some diggers can reach up to 100 metres in height – that's as tall as the Statue of Liberty.

An excavator can demolish tall buildings, too. It has a very long arm that can reach up to the top of the building.

The excavator's driver controls which way the building falls down.

Sucking up waste

A suction excavator has a special **hose** to suck up waste. It can be used to remove soil from a hole, or water from a river or a swimming pool.

A suction excavator is useful for cleaning **sewage pipes**. It can also clean up river banks without scraping away any of the land.

A suction excavator works fast. The hose could empty a bath in only four minutes!

This machine works like a vacuum cleaner to suck up waste into the truck.

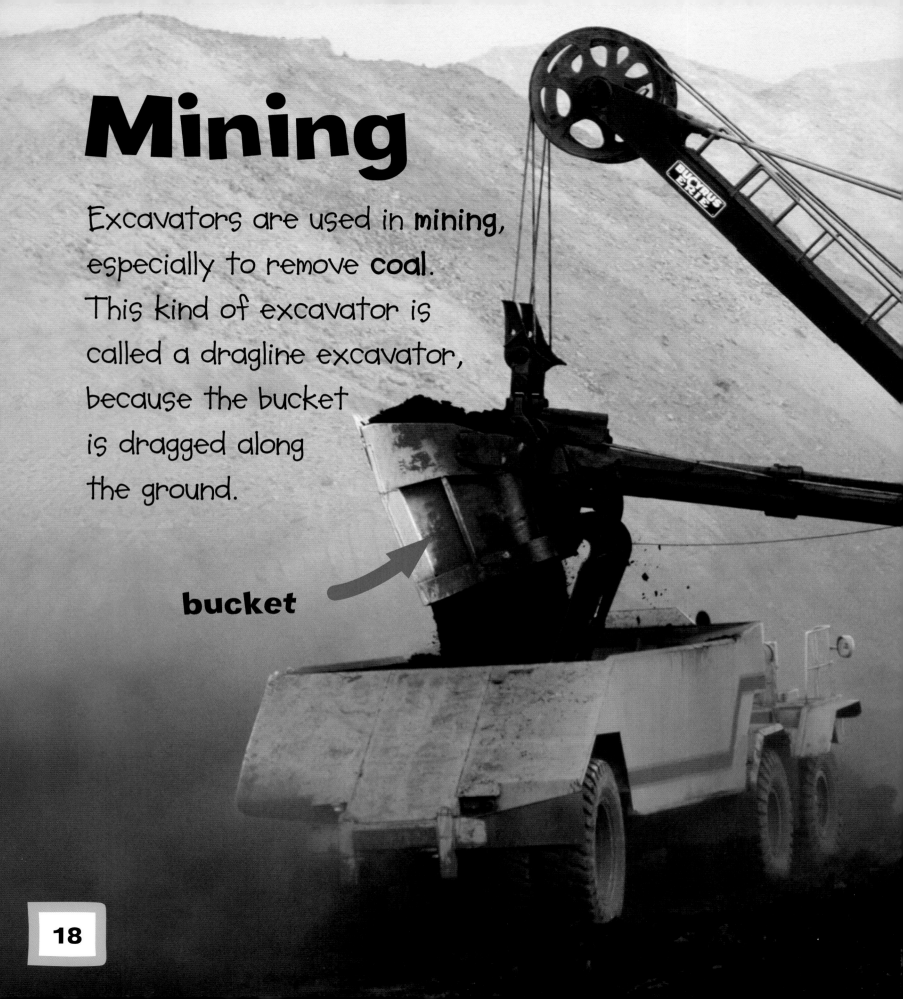

Mining

Excavators are used in **mining**, especially to remove **coal**. This kind of excavator is called a dragline excavator, because the bucket is dragged along the ground.

bucket

18

The bucket is moved by steel ropes. One of the ropes moves the bucket up and down. Other ropes move it from side to side.

steel ropes

arm

utility
coals (1978) ltd.

195-B

Biggest and smallest

The biggest excavator in the world works in coal mines. It is called Bagger 288 and it weighs 45,500 tonnes. That is the same weight as 550 passenger planes.

This monster machine can move 240,000 tonnes of coal a day. This is the same weight as 40,000 elephants or 3000 passenger planes.

There are many mini-excavators. They are used in gardens to clear garden waste or for small building jobs.

This is one of the smallest mini-excavators!

Activities

- Can you name these three attachments from the book? Can you remember what each one does?

- An excavator can knock down a building. Why is it a good machine to use?

- Draw a building site with as many diggers as you could use. Which ones did you choose? What colour are they?

- Which picture shows a suction excavator?

Glossary

Attachment
A tool on the end of a digger's arm. The tool is usually a bucket.

Bucket
A large container on the end of a digger's arm. It is used to scoop up earth and stones.

Building site
A place where a house or other building is being built.

Bulldozer
A tractor with a blade on the front. It is used to push earth and rubble.

Coal
A hard, black rock that is dug out of the ground. We burn it mainly to make electricity.

Demolish
To knock down a building.

Hose
A long pipe or tube.

Loader
A tractor with a large bucket on the front.

Mining
Taking coal out of the ground.

Rubble
Broken stones or bricks, usually on a building site.

Sewage pipe
A pipe that takes away waste from people's homes and offices.

Index